Coconut Oil and My Dog: Natural Pet Health for My Canine Friend

BJ Richards

D1607830

Copyright © 2017, BJ Richards

ISBN: 978-1513628578

Disclaimer

Legal Notice: - BJ Richards and the accompanying materials have used their best efforts in preparing the material. This book has been composed with the best intention of providing correct and reliable information. The information provided is offered solely for informational purposes and is universal as so. This information is presented without contract or any type of guarantee assurance.

BJ Richards makes no representation or warranties with respect to the accuracy, applicability, fitness or completeness of the contents of this book. The information contained in this book is strictly for educational purposes. Therefore, if you wish to apply ideas contained in this book, you are taking full responsibility for your actions.

BJ Richards disclaims any warranties (express or implied), merchantability, or fitness for any particular purpose. BJ Richards shall in no event be held liable to any party for any direct, indirect, punitive, special, incidental or other consequential damages arising directly or indirectly from any use of this material, which is provided "as is", and without warranties.

Any and all trademarks used in this book are owned by the owners themselves, are not affiliated with this book and for clarifying purposes only.

As always, the advice of a competent medical, legal, tax, accounting or other professional should be sought. BJ Richards does not warrant the performance, effectiveness or applicability of any sites listed or linked to in this book. All links are for information purposes only and are not warranted for content, accuracy or any other implied or explicit purpose.

This book is not intended as a substitute for the medical advice of physicians or veterinarians. The reader should regularly consult a physician or veterinarian in matters relating to his/her health or the health of their pet and particularly with respect to any symptoms that may require diagnosis or medical attention.

Dedication

This book would not have been possible if not for the encouragement of the fur children who kept me laughing and helped me take a break when it was needed. Thank you, Simon, Chloe, Rudy and Elsa. You kept me smelling the roses.

And to my loving daughter who is so proud of me for becoming an author.

TABLE OF CONTENTS

Introduction...8

Who's Been Using Coconut Oil and Why...9

Why Use Coconut Oil...........................15

The Components of Coconut Oil...........17

The Different Kinds of Fats and
Hydrogenated Oils..........................23

What is a Saturated Fat?....................32

Which Kind of Coconut Oil is the Right
Kind?..39

How Much Coconut Oil to Give Your
Dog..47

Conditions and Coconut Oil Uses...........53

Controlling Fleas and Ticks.................53

Digestive Ailments and Conditions.........55

Parasites and Giardia..........................58

Bone Health, the Immune System and
Metabolic Health.............................59

Yeast Infections..................................61

Reduce and Prevent Doggy Odor.............66

Blood Sugar Regulations...........................68

Weight Control and Energy......................70

Brain Health.....................................72

Skin Conditions..................................73

More Tips...78

Conclusion.......................................80

Thank You...82

Introduction

I've kept this book short, without skimping on content, so you can get what you want and need without having to research hundreds of sites online and spend days pouring through the thousands of articles out there.

My objective is to give you a clear, concise overview of coconut oil and how to easily use it for your dog's best advantage. I've condensed the volumes of information out there down to an easy-to-read-and-digest format, so you can get to the information you need right away, thus helping your dog immediately.

Who's Been Using Coconut Oil

and Why

This chapter will give you a brief overview of cultures that have been using coconut oil, as well as how it's used today.

Coconut oil has been used by humans throughout history. One of the most common uses of coconut oil is for cooking. It's also a common component in make-up, cosmetics, lotions and nutraceuticals. Many have found it helpful in the treatment of yeast infections and hair treatments as well.

There are some countries such as Thailand, Sri Lanka, India and the Philippines that have a long-standing history when it comes to the use of coconut oil.

It was also quite popular in the United States and Canada until 1954, when it's popularity died out due to the release of incorrect studies. Those studies erroneously labeled the fats in coconut oil as unhealthy. But that's because the study didn't differentiate between the different types of fats and their roles in the body.

But that has changed now that the error has been corrected. We now know that some of the saturated fats are not only healthy, but essential for a body to function. Those are the kinds of fats found in coconut oil.

Were coconut oil not such an effective and inexpensive product, we wouldn't be using it as widely as we do, and have done for centuries.

Many of you may already be using coconut oil for yourselves. If you're using the right kind of coconut oil, there's no need to go out and buy another kind that is labeled "just for pets". In this case, what is good for you is good for them. You can continue to use the same coconut oil you've already purchased and have sitting in your kitchen now.

Almost everyone is looking for an alternative route to helping our pets and helping ourselves at the same time. There are many conditions that are chronic and not life threatening, that can be dealt with if you have the information and resources available to you. That's what this book is all about.

Coconut oil can also be a valuable asset to your dog, as well as yourself. The nutritional factors in coconut oil are just as helpful to dogs as they are to humans. Many feel it is the oil of the coconut that is the most nutritious and beneficial component of the coconut. In fact, many veterinarians are recommending the home use of coconut oil because it does have such high nutritional value.

Did you know that coconut oil is antifungal, antibacterial and antimicrobial? That it helps in treating a wide variety of ailments such as skin infections, poor digestion and weak immune systems? Our dogs go through many of the same conditions we do. And coconut oil can help them with all these issues, as well as the more specific canine ones. I'll be talking about all of that as we go through this book.

Most dogs love the taste of coconut oil and readily gobble it right up. This makes giving the recommended dosage quite easy and pleasant for both you and your dog.

One of the biggest challenges to owning pets, is the cost. We love them dearly and want to do the best for them we can, but we also need to do that in an economical way.

Many people are living day-to-day, paycheck-to-paycheck and often times struggling to stay healthy themselves. It can be a big job just to pay for our own medical bills. More often than not, Veterinarian bills are just as expensive as human medical bills. Plus, there's the consideration of taking time from work and the everyday schedule to deal with veterinary visits. It can become a costly, time consuming process.

In this book, I'm going to give you as much information as I have, in an easy to read and understand format, so you can make healthy choices for you and your pets without the cost and time associated with veterinary visits.

One of the easy, accessible, low cost products available on the market today to help you take control of you and your pet's health, is coconut oil. But not just any coconut oil. I'll be showing you which kind of coconut oil to buy and which ones to stay away from and why, later on in this book.

I'm also going to show you the best ways for you to use coconut oil for your dog and how to apply it in a safe, easy way. Plus, you'll be learning just how coconut oil helps your pet fight off chronic disease and coconut oil's overall contribution to improving the health and well-being for your canine companion.

You'll be taking an important step in helping your pet without additives and strange side-effects that are often associated with drugs and medication. While we still need to seek the proper medical attention for our dogs when it is needed, we can do a lot at home with far less expense once we understand what to do and why. As always, go see your vet if you have any concerns at all.

We've just covered who has been using coconut oil and why they've been using it. Now let's find out why you should use coconut oil.

WHY USE COCONUT OIL?

In this chapter, you're going to learn why it's beneficial to use coconut oil, the components of coconut oil that make it so valuable, and how that applies to your dog.

The benefits for dogs are very similar to the benefits for humans when it comes to coconut oil. I'm a strong proponent of coconut oil and have written a separate book on it called: *Coconut Oil Breakthrough: Boost Your Brain, Burn the Fat, Build Your Hair.*

That book focuses on coconut oil for humans. Here, I'm going to narrow the focus and go more into the details of the benefits of coconut oil for our dogs, though many of these benefits will also apply to other animals, as well.

One of the things I use coconut oil for is my hair. Since I've been using it, my hair is now starting to grow and not break off. I'd been trying to get past a particular length for years, but to no avail. Once I started consuming coconut oil, that changed. My hair is stronger, healthier and shinier now.

What coconut oil has done for my hair, it also does for the fur of a dog. Many owners have reported their dog's coat getting its luster back and the coat filling out where there were once thin spots.

And that's just one of the things I use it for. It helps to control my weight, alleviate food cravings and moisturize and soften my skin. And it's great for eczema-type breakouts, as well. I could go on and on, but I cover all that in my other book.

The point is, all the things that make coconut oil safe and healthy for you, also make it safe and healthy for your dog, providing your dog doesn't have an allergy to it. When it comes to giving anything to our furry friends, the same safety considerations apply to them that we would apply to ourselves.

The Components of Coconut Oil
To get a handle on why virgin coconut oil is so important to you and your dog, it's helpful to understand the makeup of coconut oil.

Did you know that coconut oil is about ninety percent saturated fat? That's why many classify it as a super food. The saturated fats found in coconut oil contain something called medium-chain triglycerides. They are powerful ingredients that provide a huge number of benefits to your dog. They help to build up the immune system, improve digestion and give a healthy coat and improved skin. I have an entire chapter devoted specifically to the saturated fats and we'll be covering them in greater detail then.

Dogs that live in the wild naturally eat diets that are high in saturated fats. That's how their bodies are designed to work. Coconut oil is full of those good fats. By giving your dog coconut oil, you're automatically mimicking their natural diet.

Lauric acid is a key component in the saturated fats found in coconut oil. In fact, 40% of the saturated fat in coconut is lauric acid. Why is this important?

Lauric acid is highly antimicrobial and antiviral. That gives it an antiseptic quality. Your body and your dog's will convert the lauric acid to a substance called monolaurin.

A study was performed in 1982 by Hierholzer and Kabara (http://www.monoclean.com/MonoLaurin_Technical_Info.pdf). The results showed that monolaurin has viricidal effects on RNA and DNA viruses. They also reported that lauric acid will help to destroy microbes such as bacteria, yeast, fungi and other pathogenic microorganisms.

Other acids found in coconut oil include palmitic acid, caprylic acid, capric acid and myristic acid. These are also medium-chain fatty acids and contribute to the anti-viral properties in coconut oil. Caprylic acid and capric acid are known for their abilities to treat fungal infections, such as ringworm, candida and thrush. But all of these are found in a lesser concentration than lauric acid.

While there are other components in virgin coconut oil, these are the most important ones:

1. Monounsaturated fatty acids: These are good fats and a healthy alternative to trans fats and refined polyunsaturated fats that are usually found in many of today's processed foods. Here are some of the benefits of monounsaturated fats that were found in a study in Sweden (http://archinte.ama-assn.org/cgi/content/abstract/158/1/41):

- Aided in weight loss.
- Reduced cholesterol levels.
- Lessened the severity of stiffness and pain for those afflicted with rheumatoid arthritis.
- Decreased the risk of breast cancer.
- Lowered the risk of stroke and heart disease.

2. <u>Poly-Phenols</u>: These are phytochemicals. That means they're found abundantly in fruits and vegetables. There are over 8000 of them that have been identified so far and they have a wide range of benefits. Here are just a few:
- Support normal blood sugar levels.
- Support brain health and fight dementia.
- Reduce inflammation.
- Protect the cardiovascular system.
- Fight cancer cells and free radicals.

Remember, these benefits are also applying to your dog, which is our focus here. Those are some pretty powerful benefits from one simple little oil.

Most dogs love the taste of coconut oil. They view it as a treat and something special, so it's normally quite easy to give them the appropriate amount (we'll be going into that in a later chapter). For those that are finicky eaters, you can easily mix it in with their food and they'll readily eat it that way without any more fuss.

I know many of you have heard about using fish oils as a source of oil for dogs. The problem with that is the mercury that many fish oils are full of. Fish eat the chemical pollutants found in the rivers and streams, which means those same pollutants are in fish oil.

Virgin coconut oil does not contain any harmful chemicals such as mercury, so that's never a concern for your dog's health.

Now you understand the basic makeup of coconut oil and how that helps your dog maintain a stronger body. Up next we'll delve into the different kinds of fats and how the right kind fat can help your dog stay healthy and further improve their lifestyle.

The Different Kinds of Fats and Hydrogenated Oil

In this chapter, we're going to cover why fats are important, the different kinds of fats and which kind is best for your dog's health.

There's been a lot of talk about the different kinds of fats. We hear people talk about good fats and bad fats. But just what does that really mean to you and your dog?

Simply put, there are fats that are difficult for the body to utilize so they get stored as excess fat. That excess fat in turn can cause a number of problems. Some of those problems include diabetes, lack of energy, exhausted organs and heart and cardiovascular problems, to name just a few. These are often times the result of the bad fats. The bad fats come from some seed and vegetable oils and hydrogenated oils.

The good fats are those fats that are easily utilized by the body for fuel and energy. Your canine companion needs a readily available supply of these, as do you. This is where virgin coconut oil comes in.

We now know that not all saturated fats are the same. Coconut oil contains a type of saturated fat known as medium-chain triglycerides (MCTs) or medium-chain fatty acids (MCFAs). The body uses MCFAs more effectively because they're shorter in length than long-chain fatty acids found in hydrogenated oil and some vegetable and seed oils.

Medium-chain fatty acids (MCFAs) bypass the intestinal tract and are handled in the liver instead. The liver then immediately converts the MCFAs into energy. This is a very quick process and makes less strain on the pancreas and digestive tract and uses fewer body resources. That newly converted energy now becomes a valuable source of fuel for your dog's body. Plus, it increases the retention of nutritional components needed for body functions.

Virgin coconut oil is so valuable to you and your dog because over ninety percent of it is made up of these good fats. Your dog's body needs the MCFAs to work properly. These are not your typical fats. They won't clog the arteries like hydrogenated fats will.

MCTs (or MCFAs) are very different from long-chain fatty acids contained in hydrogenated oils or hydrogenated fats. The fats in hydrogenated oils are very difficult for the body to utilize. That's why the body will just store them as fat and move on to its other functions. It takes too much energy from the body to try to process them. This is the kind of fat most of us refer to as "stubborn fat"; it's very difficult to get rid of. Now you know why.

So, what is it about processed hydrogenated fats that makes them so bad for us and our pets?

Hydrogenated oils started out as oils that, if left in their natural state, are actually good for you. But they have a very short shelf life. So, manufacturers put them through a chemical process that extended that shelf life. To do that, they put them under several atmospheres of pressure and heated them to temperatures of 500 to 1000 degrees.

After the heating process, they then injected the oil with a metal catalyst like platinum, aluminum or nickel. They do this to the oil for several hours so it absorbs the metal into its molecular structure. This makes the oil stay in a solid or semi-solid state at room temperature and creates an oil that is either fully hydrogenated or partially hydrogenated.

At this point this oils are closer plastic and cellulose than oil. From a chemical standpoint, hydrogenated oil is only one molecule away from being classified as a plastic. Manufacturers love this. All the enzymatic properties of the oil have been removed and the oil is now acting as preservative.

Just like plastics, hydrogenated oils can last for years and never break down. Using un-hydrogenated oils means the foods will eventually spoil, which shortens the shelf life. That costs manufacturers money. So, they use hydrogenated oils to extend shelf life and reduce manufacturing costs.

What happens when you consume foods that have been made with hydrogenated oils? Your body is trying to digest a plastic-like substance. Plastics cannot be digested and utilized by your body or your dog's body. You have now introduced a foreign substance in your diets. That foreign substance can cause a dramatic decrease in the body's ability to defend itself against disease and the immune system becomes impaired. Diseases now have a much easier time taking over the health and well-being of you and your dog's bodies

The body will continue to try to digest these hydrogenated oils. It will send more and more digestive enzymes into the stomach in an effort to break down the plastic-like nature of the hydrogenated oils. Now the internal temperature of the stomach rises, which can set off a chain of additional health issues.

And what happens to the blood? When you or your pet consume hydrogenated oils, the blood will become thicker and more viscous, just like the plastic-like oil you're eating. Now the heart has to work harder to move the thicker blood.

Blood affected by the hydrogenated oil is just thicker, it's stickier. Now it gets stuck in the arteries much easier and contributes to the arterial plaque. Studies show these oils are actually scarring the internal walls of the arteries. That's because of the nickel that is used in the hydrogenation process. The body will respond by producing cholesterol in an attempt to heal the scarring. The end result is plaque build-up on arterial walls.

Consistent consumption of the hydrogenated oils causes continuous scarring and plaque build-up in layers. The arteries become more and more narrow and the blood has a more difficult time moving through. The heart is working harder and being worn down much faster, leading to heart attack and other cardiovascular disease.

At this point the brain can become affected. The heart has a more difficult time pumping the needed blood into the head. By slowing the micro-circulation of the blood to the brain, muddled thinking and a myriad of brain related conditions can occur.

Remember how we talked about aluminum being one of the metals manufacturers use in the hydrogenation process? Research has proven that aluminum has been linked to the onset of Alzheimer's disease

This can all happen within a relatively short amount of time. Studies have shown these effects start within a few minutes of consuming anything with hydrogenated oils in them. This is just one of the ways that hydrogenated oils are contributing to heart disease and high blood pressure for you and your pets.

On top of all that, hydrogenated oils create free radicals when they are heated. Free radicals are well known as the root cause of many of today's health problems, for both humans and pets.

Free radicals cause damage to the good cells by stealing their electrons in a process called oxidation. When the free radicals oxidize the good cells, the good cells lose the ability to function properly and begin to break down. This leads to disease in the body on many different levels and can affect the brain, nervous system and all the organs.

Coconut oil does not produce free radicals when it is heated, and therefore does not destroy your dog's body (or yours), as foods containing hydrogenated oils will. In fact, coconut oil will remain stable, even at high temperatures. That's why it's safe to cook with coconut oil versus other types of oil that lose their stability at higher cooking temperatures.

Now you understand why you hear people say hydrogenated oils are not good for you or your pets. By consuming them you're actually breaking your body down on a cellular level. That's why it's important you read labels and avoid anything that is hydrogenated.

You just learned what to look for when reading labels for you and your dog to make sure you're not getting an oil that will cause disease and ill health. But we need to know a little more detail specifically on saturated fats. That's up next.

What is a Saturated Fat?

Up till now, we've covered the good fats and the bad fats. But we still need a little more clarification on the whole saturated fats issue. Where do they come from and what about them makes them a good fat? That's what this chapter is about.

Virgin coconut oil is high in saturated fats. That makes it a healthy and helpful fat and beneficial to you and your dog's bodies. This is in direct contrast to a number of other oils that are detrimental, such as the hydrogenated oils and some of the seed and vegetable oils.

On October 22, 2010, Dr. Mercola published an article on his website. This is what it said:

"It may be surprising for you to realize that the naturally occurring saturated fat in coconut oil actually has some amazing health benefits, such as:

- *Promoting your heart health.*
- *Promoting weight loss, when needed.*
- *Supporting your immune system health.*
- *Supporting a healthy metabolism.*

- *Providing you with an immediate energy source.*
- *Keeping your skin healthy and youthful looking.*
- *Supporting the proper functioning your thyroid gland.*

But how is this possible? Does coconut oil have some secret ingredient not found in other saturated fats? The answer is a resounding "yes.""

So, what is this secret ingredient Dr. Mercola was talking about? It's lauric acid.

Lauric acid comprises fifty percent of the fat content in coconut oil. But what does lauric acid do for your dog and for you that is so important?

Bodies are amazing things. They're actually chemical factories. They have the ability to change once substance into another. For example, your dog consumes virgin coconut oil that has lauric acid in it, and his body changes that into monolaurin.

Monolaurin is a substance proven to destroy the outer lipid coating on viruses. Many substances can't do that, which is why it can be so difficult to kill a virus. But, monolaurin can.

We're talking about the ability to disable viruses like herpes, measles, the flu, etc. That makes monolaurin a valuable asset to your dog's health. Instead of catching diseases like another dog might catch, your dog remains strong and healthy because you added virgin coconut oil to his diet. And it does the same thing for you. Very smart!

The other fact you'll need to understand about the saturated fats found in virgin coconut oil is about the chain length of the fatty acids it contains. Almost two-thirds of the saturated fats found in virgin coconut oil are medium-chain fatty acids (MCFAs), also known as medium-chain triglycerides (MCTs). Those are two names for the same thing, so don't let that trip you up. Anytime you see either of those terms, MCFAs or MCTs, you'll know we're talking about the same thing.

Many seed and vegetable oils and all hydrogenated oils are different from virgin coconut oil. They're made up of something known as long-chain fatty acids (LCFAs), or long-chain triglycerides (LCTs). Again, both of these terms mean exactly the same thing.

Which one is better for animals and humans? The medium-chain fatty acids or the long-chain fatty acids?

The body has a difficult time digesting and utilizing long-chain fatty acids, so here's what can happen when you or your dog eat them:

- They put stress and strain on your liver, pancreas and digestive system.
- They can be left in the arteries as cholesterol and cause blockages.
- They require the body to produce special enzymes to try to break them down. That calls for extra energy the body could be using to repair itself instead, so the body's valuable energy resource gets wasted on something it has a difficult time utilizing in the end.
- They usually end up getting stored as stubborn fat, causing more strain on the organs, decreased mobility and less energy for activity and living.

Now contrast that to what happens when you take in medium-chain fatty acids found in virgin coconut oil:

- They bypass the digestive tract and are sent directly to the liver where they're immediately converted into energy.
- They are easily digested, need far less energy to process and relieve the strain on the digestive tract.
- Your dog's metabolism gets boosted, helping them to lose weight if needed and burn off unwanted fat.
- They're a much smaller molecule, so they pass through the cellular membranes easily, without the need for special enzymes. This means the body can put them to work right away.

When you contrast the two, it becomes obvious that medium-chain fatty acids are healthy and helpful to your dog, whereas long-chain fatty acids can cause a number of health problems. Now you understand why giving your dog virgin coconut oil and not foods containing the seed and vegetable oils with long-chain fatty acids, is a good thing to do.

We've just learned what makes saturated fats so powerful and why you and your dog need them in your daily diets. But what about the different kinds of coconut oil? What's the right one to buy? I cover that in the next chapter.

Which Kind of Coconut Oil is the Right Kind?

One of the big questions I get asked is which type of coconut oil should I be buying? We'll cover that now in detail.

There are several different kinds of coconut oil on the market. You want to give your dog the same kind of coconut oil that you would consume. That means virgin coconut oil.

Coconut oil falls into two main categories:

1. Refined: This is highly processed and industrially mass produced.
2. Coconut oil from fresh coconuts: This type is far less refined and is exactly what we're looking for.

Since coconuts grow on trees and the coconut oil is inside the coconut, it is already a refined product, but naturally refined. You can't tap a coconut and have the oil just run out, it has to be extracted. Which means the only truly "unrefined" coconut oil is still inside the coconut meat.

So just what is "virgin" coconut oil, anyway and how do you get it out of the coconut meat?

In the early 2000s the term "virgin coconut oil" was coined by the coconut industries in the Philippines to distinguish the lesser refined coconut oil from the highly-refined coconut oil.

Highly refined coconut oil starts out as copra. Copra is dried coconut meat that has been removed from the shell, then subjected to extreme processes. Due to the processes used to produce copra, it is inedible. Copra is its own product and is usually sold to manufacturing companies where they refine it even further.

Copra drying processes can be accomplished through a number of different avenues such as kiln, smoke, sun, or a combination thereof. By the time the product reaches this point it is dirty and smoky and not safe for consumption. The copra is then further refined to produce an industrial grade of coconut oil.

Many highly-refined coconut oils are labeled as RBD. Coconut oils labeled as RBD are oils which have been refined, bleached and deodorized. The bleaching will remove impurities and uses a bleaching clay. That is then deodorized. The end product is an oil without odor or taste or nutritional value.

You can understand why you wouldn't want your dog to consume anything manufactured by these processes.

Here are the different types of coconut oils that are out on the market today:

Hydrogenated Coconut Oil: These are not oils you want to consume. These have been processed so the unsaturated fatty acids are hydrogenated, meaning they will stay solid at higher temperatures. This makes them unusable by the body.

Coconut Oil: If it doesn't say "virgin coconut oil" and has no other description other than "coconut oil" on the label, it's probably RBD. Companies that produce copra export it to countries around the world, including the U.S., where it's further refined to produce cleaning products, detergents, etc.

In the wake of increasing popularity of coconut oil use, some of these companies are now starting to produce coconut oil for internal consumption. They are usually cheaper and are probably mass produced with solvent extracts.

Whether or not the solvent extracts remain in the finished product is difficult to say. If you purchase this type of product, you'll want to read the label thoroughly and make sure it wasn't produced with any type of solvent.

Liquid Coconut Oil: We started seeing coconut oil hit the market in 2013 with this type of labeling. The benefit being touted was that it would remain a liquid, even when refrigerated. This is actually fractionated coconut oil, and is not a new product at all.

Fractionated coconut oil has had all the lauric acid removed, hence all the antibacterial, antiviral and antifungal properties are gone. Some have coined this type of oil as "MCT oil", meaning medium-chain triglyceride oil. It used to be you only saw this used for skin care products. Now, some companies are selling it as an edible dietary supplement.

MCT oil is nothing more than a byproduct of the lauric acid industry. As we've talked about before, it is the lauric acid that has the antipathogenic properties. These properties make lauric acid a viable commercial preservative.

Lauric acid makes up almost fifty percent of coconut oil. When removed from the coconut oil, the melting point is lowered, making it easier to process. So be aware, when you find this type of coconut oil on the shelves, it's missing the all-important lauric acid and antimicrobial properties.

<u>Virgin Coconut Oils</u>: Are there different kinds? If it says "virgin coconut oil", it should've started out as fresh coconut, not copra. But, as of now, I haven't found any agency that certifies this to be true. Which means, if you're not buying from a reputable source, you may not be getting true virgin coconut oil.

Virgin coconut oil will be a solid at temperatures of 76 degree Fahrenheit and below and have a coconut smell and taste. But it will melt at temperatures above that. So, if it's sitting out on your kitchen counter in the summer, it will go to a liquid state.

<u>Extra Virgin Coconut Oil</u>: This is not different from "virgin coconut oil". Extra virgin coconut oil is a labeling device used in

marketing; there are no real differences between the two.

To make sure you're getting the right kind of coconut oil for your dog, make sure what you're buying says "virgin" coconut oil on the label and you're buying from a reputable company. If you're not sure, then move on. There are too many benefits to be gained from having your dogs consume the right kind, and too much to lose from having them consume the wrong kind.

Stability of Virgin Coconut Oil: One of the great things about virgin coconut oil is its stability. Unlike other oils that may go rancid after a few weeks or months, virgin coconut oil will stay fresh and useable for extended periods of time. Virgin coconut oil has been known to last for years past the "best by" date.

If you're not sure if your virgin coconut oil is still good or not, use your senses. If something smells rancid or shows signs of mold, then it's time to get rid of it.

Refined coconut oil has a much shorter shelf life, only about two to three months. Hopefully, you're not using that version of coconut oil for your pet or yourself. But it would be fine as a lubricant on squeaky hinges, etc.

You just learned which specific type of coconut oil you want to buy for consumption by you and your canine friend. But we need to know how much to give. That's what the next chapter is all about.

How Much Coconut Oil to Give Your Dog

One thing we need to know is how much virgin coconut oil to give to our pets and how to apply it to skin conditions. That's what we're going to cover now.

A conservative approach is always recommended. As with anything that is new and being introduced into your dog's diet, you want to start slowly.

One approach is to mix the coconut oil with your dog's food and use the lower recommended dosage. You can increase it a little at a time, providing there are no adverse side effects, such as finding out your dog is allergic to coconut oil. While this is less likely, it is a possibility, so exercise caution in the beginning.

Too much too fast can cause a detox reaction. Remember, coconut oil will kill pathogens. You want the die-off to be a slow process, not a fast debilitating one. Detox symptoms can include diarrhea and greasy stools, fatigue, lethargy, even flu-like symptoms.

Give your pet's body a chance to deal with the expulsion of the pathogens. Start small.

- A quarter-teaspoon each day for puppies and smaller dogs is sufficient.
- For large dogs, one teaspoon per day will suffice.
- If your dog's digestive system is sensitive, you can start with even smaller amounts.
- After your dog has been successfully introduced to virgin coconut oil for several days, you can begin to increase the amount. The general guideline is about one teaspoon per ten to twenty pounds of body weight, every day. Or about one tablespoon per thirty pounds. DO NOT START WITH THESE HIGHER AMOUNTS. Start out with the smaller amounts listed above.
- If you're trying to treat a specific condition, you can try one teaspoon for every five pounds of weight, but ONLY after your dog has gotten through the adaptation period.

If your dog's attitude changes and you notice they're getting worn out easily or grumpy, immediately reduce the amount. Stay at the lower dosage temporarily. You can also divide up the lowered dosage into even smaller amounts spread throughout the day.

It's best to start them out by mixing it in with their food, or offering it to them at the same time they eat. Since most dogs will lick it right off your fingers, let them eat first, then lick the amount you're giving them from your hand.

If your dog likes this method, it's one way you're sure they're getting the amount you're feeding. If it's mixed in with the food and they don't eat it all, you have no way of knowing how much they really consumed. But it's certainly fine to mix it in with the food if they don't want to lick it out of your hand. If you want to pre-liquefy it, you can put the prescribed amount in a small cup and set that in some hot water. It will liquefy right away.

Since most dogs like the taste of coconut oil, giving it to them will not be a stressful ordeal. As always, exercise common sense and good judgement. You know your dog better than anyone. If your dogs are overweight, they will require a little more coconut oil. A dog that is fit and healthy, will require less. Puppies grow quickly, so they may not need as long a period of time to adapt.

And be aware that while coconut oil is good for the digestion, too much can cause loose stools. So again, err on the side of caution and start slowly with the smaller amounts. You can also add a little canned pumpkin to their food if this happens. Pumpkin is well known for its ability to regulate stools, either too hard or too soft.

Topical Application: Since coconut oil is so safe, you can apply it directly to their skin if you're treating a skin issue. You may need to wrap the area with a cloth to keep them from licking it, but just until it soaks in, which only takes a few minutes. Dilution isn't necessary for most pets.

Precautions: While very few dogs are allergic to coconut oil, the possibility still exists. Be sure to start out with the recommended doses and go slowly.

If your dog exhibits an allergic reaction, stop immediately. Also, some vets warn against giving a dog coconut oil if they have pancreatitis due to its high fat content.

If you dog has high cholesterol or obesity issues, consult your vet before making any changes in their diet.

Disclaimer: Consult your dog's medical professional with all questions and concerns or before adding anything new to their regimen.

You just learned how much virgin coconut oil to give your dog, what side effects could occur and how to apply it to skin conditions. What we want to talk about next is how to use it for specific conditions. That's the next chapter.

Conditions and Coconut Oil Uses

There are many conditions your dog may be dealing with and you want to know how virgin coconut oil can help. That's what we're covering in this chapter.

Listed here are several conditions that coconut oil may help to heal and control. Be sure to use the application guidelines discussed in the previous chapter on "how to give and apply" coconut oil. And again, while very few dogs are allergic, the possibility does exist. If you see allergic reactions, discontinue immediately. And once again, if your pet has pancreatitis, some vets warn against giving them coconut oil due to its high fat content. Be sure to consult your vet before proceeding.

Controlling Fleas and Ticks:
All dogs love to romp and play, especially in the summertime. Unfortunately, that's also the time when fleas and ticks abound.

Uncontrolled fleas and ticks can cause your dog to suffer:

- Dermatitis and skin infections
- Scratching and biting the skin

- Hair loss
- Scabs and hot spots
- Tape worms

Yes, there are products you can get from several manufacturers, but the chemical cocktails they use are actually toxic to your dog. For example, the drug in Frontline is fipronil. Research has shown fipronil has side effects that can cause cancer, nervous system damage, seizures, rashes, skin problems and reproductive damage. And they're not the only company whose flea and tick control products have these side effects. All such products use chemicals that are toxic to animals.

When seeking a natural flea and tick control alternative, you don't want to use Garlic, either. It can function like a poison if consumed in large enough quantities, so that is definitely not a viable solution.

Virgin coconut oil, however, is completely safe and can stop your dog from needlessly suffering the ravages of fleas and ticks. Why? Because the insect repellant in virgin coconut oil that repels fleas and ticks is lauric acid, proven safe for animals and humans.

<u>To apply:</u> Rub about a half-teaspoon or less between your palms, depending on your dog's size. Then rub that onto their legs, stomach, higher and lower back. In the beginning, you may need to apply each time they go for a walk. But eventually, you may only need to apply once to twice per day.

What a safe and easy way to save your dog from suffering, and to stop paying the exorbitant prices of the flea repellant manufacturers.

Digestive Ailments and Conditions:

Virgin coconut oil is one of the best natural sources you can find for medium-chain triglycerides (MCTs) also known as medium-chain fatty acids. Because they are smaller, they are absorbed more easily into the digestive system. The long-chained fatty acids are found in oils like vegetable and seed oils and hydrogenated oil and are more difficult for your pet to absorb.

That means the MCTs will absorb quickly and easily and will also help other nutrients that are needed to be absorbed quicker and easier, also. The antifungal and antimicrobial nature of the virgin coconut oil ensures these other nutrients are absorbed without destroying them or without the other oils and nutrients causing a bacterial interaction within the intestinal tract.

Vitamins and minerals are then more fully absorbed and utilized by your pet's body. That means your dog receives more benefit from the food and supplements you're already giving them.

Have you ever noticed fatty deposits in the stools of your dog? That's because some of the fats they tried to consume were not absorbed adequately. If your dog's colon is not operating as efficiently as it could, those long-chain fatty acids will not be absorbed and be excreted in the stools. Virgin coconut oil will help your dog to absorb the needed requirements from those long-chain fatty acids.

Be sure you're cooking your dog's food in virgin coconut oil and not olive oil. Olive oil has a low smoke point. A low smoke point means it will incur oxidative damage and can produce harmful compounds when heated. Virgin coconut oil is more stable at higher temperatures and therefore safer for cooking for you and your pet.

Cooking with virgin coconut oil is an important step in improving the digestive abilities of your dog's intestinal tract and helping to prevent digestive related problems like Irritable Bowel Syndrome, gas and nausea.

It is the antiparasitic qualities in virgin coconut oil that will help to combat all the various forms of bacteria and fungi that can cause indigestion. If you see that your dog is suffering from gas and bloating after eating due to poor digestion, you may want to consider adding coconut oil to their food.

The high levels of the beneficial fatty acids in the coconut oil will have a soothing effect on issues like candida, parasites and bacterias that cause intestinal digestive problems.

Parasites and Giardia:
Giardia is a common digestive ailment in dogs that affects the small intestine. Dogs that eat the feces of other dogs are most likely to deal with this. Coconut oil may provide an effective defense against this and other parasites. Research has proven the effectiveness of medium-chain fatty acids in destroying Giardia, as well as possibly ridding your dog of other harmful protozoa,

such as ringworm and tapeworms. Daily ingestion of virgin coconut oil may be the answer to stopping Giardia from ever gaining a footing in your dog's digestive system, thus keeping them from suffering from this digestive issue.

Bone Health, the Immune System and Metabolic Health:

One of the great benefits of virgin coconut oil is its ability to boost your dog's immune system. This is due to a number of inherent components found in the coconut oil: capric acid, caprylic acid, antimicrobial lipids and lauric acid. All of these contain antiviral, antimicrobial, antifungal and antibacterial properties.

Studies with humans show the human body will convert the lauric acid into a substance known as monolaurin. Monolaurin is proven to be one of the most effective components in combatting microorganisms and viruses that cause many of the illnesses that plague us and our pets such as herpes and the flu.

It is due to virgin coconut oil's high concentrations of the medium-chain fatty acids that can be converted into monolaurin that it can deal with issues like infected gums, candida, influenza and pylori (spiral-shaped bacteria that can grow in the digestive tract and destroy the intestinal lining).

The Coconut Research Center at http://coconutresearchcenter.org/, shows that coconut oil also assists in controlling measles, hepatitis and SARS. And that coconut oil eradicates the bacteria that causes throat infections, gingivitis, pneumonia, urinary tract infections and ulcers.

One of the important things to know about medium-chain fatty acids is they bypass the digestive system and are quickly converted into energy in the liver. That means a boost to the metabolic system and increase in the energy levels the body can use to function with.

Medium-chain fatty acids don't get stored in the tissue like other fats do, so they don't contribute to extra body weight. It's easier to control your dog's weight when you give them virgin coconut oil. And the increase in the metabolic processes means they're burning off unwanted stored fat quicker, but in a healthy safe way.

Remember how we talked about the ability of virgin coconut oil to help other nutrients absorb easier? That includes a faster, more effective absorption of magnesium and calcium. Magnesium and calcium are critical to building strong healthy teeth and solid bones. By including virgin coconut oil in your pet's diet, you're also decreasing their risk of dental and bone problems.

Yeast Infections:
One of the most common uses for virgin coconut oil is in the treatment and prevention of the various types of yeast infections, which includes Candida. It can offer both internal and external relief from the itching and indigestion caused by yeast. Due to its high ability to hold moisture, it can prevent the skin from peeling, then cracking open and bleeding, all common, painful side effects of yeast infected skin.

It is the lauric acid and caprylic acid in the coconut oil that have the most influence in controlling the yeast. But all of the medium-chain fatty acids in coconut oil contribute and will kill virus, bacteria and yeast overgrowth.

Laboratory tests have shown that coconut oil has the ability to shatter the Candida yeast cell nucleus, thus destroying the yeast and its overgrowth. It has also been shown to lessen the skin irritation and soreness your pet may be suffering in sensitive private areas. So be sure to use virgin coconut oil topically on these infected outside areas.

Symptoms of yeast overgrowth include your dog being lethargic, mentally foggy, unable to digest their food well and constantly getting one disease after another. That is due to their immune system being impaired by the Candida.

Many times a pet's human companion will see a significant improvement in their dog's health within a relatively short time once they start giving them virgin coconut oil. The caprylic acid in the coconut oil goes to work right away exercising its antifungal properties, thus immediately beginning to give your pet relief.

Also be aware that a pet infected with Candida should not be given regular milk, as it will worsen their symptoms. It would be wise to substitute unsweetened coconut milk, which is healthier and will help to relieve yeast overgrowth symptoms.

One thing to be aware of if your dog is suffering from a yeast infection is die-off and die-off symptoms. Because virgin coconut oil is killing the yeast, your dog's immune system has to deal with the dead yeast and other fungi that are being killed. So, you want to start off slowly with lower dosages, as recommended in the chapter on how much to take.

Die-off symptoms can be very uncomfortable and sometimes severe if the yeast is killed too quickly. Those symptoms can include nausea, vomiting, diarrhea and flu-like symptoms. But because you're using virgin coconut oil and not a pharmaceutical, your pet will have a lesser chance of experiencing these symptoms. You'll still want to be vigilant and go slowly, though.

If your pet is dealing with systemic Candida, you'll want to start out with the lesser dosages and increase them a little at a time. Systemic Candida is also known as "invasive Candida". This is a very different form of yeast infection than the Candida infections found in the mouth and throat or vagina.

Invasive/systemic Candida is a serious infection that can affect the blood, brain, eyes, heart, bones and other parts of the body. Since this is such a serious issue, you'll want to make sure you're working alongside your pet's medical professional.

There are many different reasons why the normal Candida Albicans found in the stomach of all animals becomes unregulated and out of control. Normally, it doesn't cause these kinds of severe issues. One of the reasons it can get out of control is the use of antibiotics.

Antibiotics kill the good bacteria in the gut that is needed to control the Candida and bad bacteria. Anytime you're giving your dog antibiotics you should also be giving them probiotics to counter these unwanted effects. The probiotics are concentrations of the good bacteria and yeast that every gut needs to stay healthy.

Ingesting foods full of preservatives, sugars and other toxins can also lead to a depletion of good gut bacteria. The fewer chemicals, sugars and preservatives you can give your pet through their foods and water, the better gut health and immune system they will have.

You can find probiotics for pets in most health food stores, at many vets and online. The labels on these products will tell you the proper amount to give to your dog, as well as how often and when. If you have any questions you feel these sources cannot answer for you, consult your pet's health care practitioner.

Reduce and Prevent Doggy Odor:

Another great benefit of virgin coconut oil is its ability to deal with unpleasant doggy odor.

An easy way to do this is to melt a small amount of coconut oil in your hand, add a little of your dog's shampoo to that, then give them their bath. The coconut oil will deodorize your dog's fur and skin by killing off bacteria, fungus and germs that contribute to the malodor.

If you bathe your pet on a regular basis and always use the coconut oil in with the shampoo, you'll go a long way toward ending any kind of doggie odor coming from their body. They'll stay clean and sweet smelling and your own nose will love it, too!

Virgin coconut oil smells great and will never harm your dog. So, it's a win-win for you and your pet. Once again, make sure your pet is not allergic to coconut oil before using it in any form for your canine friend.

You can also brush your dog's teeth with virgin coconut oil. It will kill off the bacteria causing the odor, thus freshening their breath and help to heal their gums at the same time. And most dogs like the taste, making the job much easier.

Blood Sugar Regulation:

When you or your dog are not able to regulate blood sugar, a number of complications can come up. These can include obesity and weight gain, constant hunger, hypoglycemia or even severe diabetic shock.

The body requires glucose in order to function and live. Glucose normally comes from the foods we eat. But these forms of glucose are made up of many long molecular structures and have difficulty entering the cells, so they need insulin to make that happen.

Coconut oil is not digested in the intestinal tract since it is a medium-chain fatty acid. Instead these medium-chain fatty acids go directly to the liver where there are immediately converted to energy. That means they are converted to energy without the body's use of insulin.

Whether you have insulin resistance or not, coconut oil still works and does its job. Coconut oil can be taken to regulate and improve the function of the pancreas where insulin is secreted from.

Your dog's body gets a metabolic boost when they consume virgin coconut oil. The medium-chain fatty acids (MCFAs) help to regulate the digestive system and improve the functioning of the thyroid. This will give your dog a higher metabolic rate, thus stimulating the pancreas to produce needed insulin when necessary. And remember, when your dog has a higher metabolism, they're also burning off unneeded fat contributing to obesity.

After you or your dog eat, blood sugar levels will usually rise, at least a little. To balance the blood sugar levels, the body calls for more insulin from the pancreas. Since the lauric acid present in virgin coconut oil helps to speed the body's metabolism, the pancreas is able to function more efficiently, thus easing its job and the energy it requires to work. This helps the pancreas recover more rapidly and prevent issues of being over worked.

Studies that were done in 1982 by Ginsbert and another in 1989 by Yost and Eckel both showed that MCFAs in coconut oil have a greater ability than other oils when it comes to increasing and developing the binding properties between insulin and the cells. What that means to you and your pet is an effective use of glucose in the body and control of insulin resistance.

Weight Control and Energy:

This is a tough one for older dogs and dogs with limited mobility. It's sometimes difficult for our canine friends to be active when they become seniors or have joint problems. And this leads to unwanted weight gain and the problems that go along with that.

Fortunately, there's virgin coconut oil. The medium-chain fatty acids will help in losing that excess weight. As we've talked about earlier, the metabolic rate is naturally increased when your dog consumes virgin coconut oil. This increased metabolism functioning, will burn off stored fat and give their cells more energy to help them heal and get through the day much easier.

That will take stress off the pancreas, help to regulate their thyroid and increase the ease and capability of their intestinal tract to digest their food more fully.

It is a known fact that in parts of the world where cultures have used coconut oil in their diet on a daily basis, they are generally not obese or overweight. That is due to the many abilities just mentioned above. What coconut oil has done for them for centuries in burning off fat and increasing metabolism, it can also do for you and your dog.

Animals that eat vegetable oils gain weight more easily. This is because vegetable oils often contain long-chain fatty acids and not medium-chain fatty acids. Long-chain fatty acids are more difficult for the body to break down and utilize, so they get stored in the body's tissues as excess fat. So, you can see why you want to avoid giving your dog foods that utilize vegetable oils instead of virgin coconut oil.

Brain Health:

There are two types of foods that can be converted by animals (including humans) into energy. Those are fats and glucose or sugars.

The body will convert fat into something called ketones. When the body has a limited supply of glucose, it will use an alternative source, which are the ketones. Medium-chain fatty acids, also known as medium-chain triglycerides, are also an important source of ketones. And we know how MCT dense virgin coconut oil is in this valuable source for your dog's body.

Ketones serve an additional role in your dog's brain (and yours). The ketones not only provide an alternative source of fuel for their brain, they also help to protect its neurons. Neurons are cells in you and your dog's nervous system that function as the brain's basic working unit. They are specially designed to transmit information to the muscles, glands and other nerve cells. You and your dog's body would not be able to function without its neurons. And those neurons need to be kept in tip-top shape.

There have been a number of studies showing how important ketones are in not only protecting neurons, but in renewing damaged neurons, repairing and restoring them. Since virgin coconut oil is so rich in MCTs, by adding it to your dog's diet, you're automatically giving them what their body needs to improve their cognitive functioning and increase their ability to function mentally on a daily basis.

Skin Conditions:

Coconut oil is one of the most healthy and soothing oils you can use for the skin. It is commonly used for massage for both animals and humans. It will moisturize the skin, helping to heal dry cracked areas and leave the skin smooth and silky.

It's the lauric acid in the coconut oil that is so powerful when it comes to treating things like rashes, dermatitis, psoriasis and eczema, as well as many of the other skin conditions listed below. That's why it's so commonly found in a number of products like soaps, shampoos and lotions. The lauric acid will immediately go to work to help heal the inflammation and allow the body to repair itself naturally.

You can use coconut oil for many different types of skin infections and conditions, so you're not limited by the type. Coconut oil will disinfect any type of cut as well, thus enabling it to heal faster.

Using coconut oil on a regular basis will provide the skin with the foundation it needs to rejuvenate and repair itself. It helps to delay common skin conditions such as sagging and the appearance of fine lines and wrinkles. Which means regular use for your canine friend will help keep them looking and feeling younger. Even our pets appreciate being beautiful!

If you're like most human pet companions, if you use coconut oil on your dog's coat on a regular basis, you'll notice a significant improvement to how shiny and healthy their coat becomes. Coconut oil will also deodorize your dog's skin, helping to control "doggie" smell.

Unlike other oils such as mineral oil, there are no adverse side effects to coconut oil.

Mineral oil is distilled from petroleum, and is not a natural oil. Also, mineral oil comes with a list of warnings and side effects. So please, do not use it on your dog or any of your pets. Stick with coconut oil so you know your dog will be safe.

For dog's dealing with hot spots or skin conditions, you can apply the coconut oil directly to the skin. They will find it soothing. Let it soak in for about five minutes. You can then rinse off any extra with warm water so they don't lick and get more than their allowed dosage if necessary.

Here is a partial list of just some of the skin conditions virgin coconut oil has been proven to help:

- Flaky skin
- Cuts
- Stings
- Bites
- Clearing dermatitis and eczema.
- Helping soften and improve the texture of skin.
- Healing cracked paws.
- Deodorizing skin and fur.
- Treating and healing bites and stings

- Healing hot spots.
- Controlling mange
- Treating and preventing itchy, dry and flaky skin.
- Rashes, psoriasis

Using Coconut Oil as a Carrier Oil: If you use high quality essential oils on your dog, you'll want to consider coconut oil as a carrier oil. Coconut oil will penetrate the skin easily and help your pet to absorb other beneficial oils that are too strong to be used as a stand-alone, but need the dilution. You can also use it as a carrier oil for herbal extracts. Most dogs like the taste of coconut oil, so mixing the herbal extracts in with the coconut oil will help them get it down without a fuss.

Coconut oil may also be of significant help in the following. This is due in part to its antiviral, antifungal and antimicrobial properties in combination with its other components.

- Preventing disease and infection.
- Helping to control allergies.

- Controlling coughing, example: kennel cough
- Relieving colitis and inflammatory bowel syndrome.
- Healing a cracked or chapped nose.
- Helping control and clear hairballs by coating their mouth and throat.
- Helping to heal gums.
- Helping to improve their heart health and cardiovascular system.
- Helping to control and treat fevers, abscesses, constipation, malnutrition, ulcers, nausea.

Here are some more tips:

Coconut oil is useful in helping to lubricate your dog's joints and ligaments, thus reducing pain in those areas.

If they need to swallow a pill, coat it with coconut oil. Most dogs love the taste and the coconut oil will help to digest it quicker. It helps any medication glide through the throat and digestive system easier, thus eliminating esophageal erosion and digestive upset.

Do you have to give your dog antibiotics? Combine it with virgin coconut oil. The antifungal properties will reduce the risk of the antibiotics giving your pet a yeast overgrowth problem. Your dog needs the healthy bacteria in their system to fight off illness and the bad bacteria.

In addition to all these great benefits, you will benefit financially since you'll save by not having to spend money on expensive medications and healthcare. And your pet will benefit by not having to suffer the side effects of traditional medications.

As always, you'll want to seek professional advice for your dog's health when it is warranted.

Conclusion

We love our pets as we love our children. They are in our lives on a daily basis. They live in our homes, sleep in our arms and give us kisses every single day.

It is vital we keep them as healthy as possible, for as long as possible. For them and for us. And we want to do that naturally without the use of chemicals and drugs, whenever we can.

That's what makes virgin coconut oil such an important tool for everyone's health, theirs and ours. When they're healthy and happy, we're also healthier and happier. Everybody wins.

Virgin coconut oil can be a great natural boost to their health, helping them to live active fulfilling lives without the side effects of so many of the drugs that are out there today. And because it's so readily obtainable, it will work its magic without breaking the bank.

While coconut oil is not a miracle, it's the closest thing to it I've found to help all of us lead a happier, healthier life. We owe it to them. We owe it to ourselves.

Coconut Oil and My Dog   BJ Richards

How does that commercial go? *We're worth it.*

Thank You

I just want to take a moment to thank you for your interest. I hope you enjoyed reading this book as much as I enjoyed writing it.

If you'd like even more information on virgin coconut oil and its health benefits, check out my book: Coconut Oil Breakthrough: Boost Your Brain, Burn the Fat, Build Your Hair.

You can connect directly with me here:

http://bjrichardsauthor.com

https://www.facebook.com/BJ.Richards.Author

CPSIA information can be obtained
at www.ICGtesting.com
Printed in the USA
LVHW050845130319
610484LV00023B/289/P

9 781513 628578